TAP INTO SOURCE

A SPIRITUAL AWAKENING EXPLAINED. THE
PATHWAY TO PEACE AND PURPOSE.

BRANDI EDWARDS

SOLEMN CREATIVES

CONTENTS

Cover Design by: Brandi Edwards

Publishing Assistance provided by:

Michelle Morrow

www.chellreads.com

I dedicate my book to the memory of Priscilla R. Stoney. My beloved aunt who guided me spiritually, both during her life and after she passed. Thank you for the prayers, the encouragement and always having faith in me. I hope I make you proud.

Dear Reader,

At different points in my life I spiritually made involuntary visits to another realm. On a few of those visits I was given the option to stay, but I always opted to return to the home that I knew. Some of the others that were in this place did not choose to return, for example, a mother had the option to return to this life, but she chose to stay with her toddler son, who could not return. For some reason God wanted me to see this, and in hindsight, I was always able to. Now that I am older and un-afraid, I have a better understanding of where I went and where WE are going.

Brandi

INTRODUCTION

One of the worst things you can do to a non-religious person is immerse them in your own religious beliefs. Some fail to realize different people hypothetically speak different languages; therefore, approach and communication is everything. I believe that religion is a vessel to strengthen your spirituality and to personally tap into the Source is the goal. Source is God, the most high, the universe, etc. Most importantly Source is LOVE. People get so hung up on titles that they forget to focus on purpose.

Tap into Source is a guide and resource regarding spiritual awakening. This book is a tool that one can refer to whenever one is searching for insight, information, reminders, encouragement, and understanding.

I detail how to cope with the symptoms of awakening

and also how to create a connection with Source. In spirituality, you will find that one must face their darkness before one can radiate their brightest light. The unknown can be scary, but once you gain understanding and a direct relationship with the divine source, you can become unstoppable. I will also explain my take on religion and how it correlates with spirituality.

Many often wonder what people mean when they speak of spiritual awakening, Kundalini energy, 3rd eye awakening, etc. Even I was clueless to what this all really meant, until I experienced my own awakening.

It is often said that people can have very different awakening experiences, but I am convinced when you truly have gone through it, you will feel it, and you will know it.

SPIRITUAL AWAKENING

Many will encounter different symptoms of awakening. Several symptoms of awakening are listed below.

- Headaches or Migraines
- Waking up between 3-4am regularly
- Having a 6th sense
- Hearing and feeling energy that you may not actually see
- Noticing shadow figures, or constantly seeing unexplainable movements in your peripheral vision
- Feeling like someone is watching you
- Hearing whispers or voices
- Having vivid and lucid dreams

- Randomly smelling beautiful or very horrid smells
- Feeling like you are being guided
- A desire to be in nature
- Dreaming of the deceased, or receiving messages from the deceased via music, signs, or symbols
- Feeling vibrations in your body, typically along your spine
- Breathing problems
- Anxiety or chest pains
- Synchronicities such as 555,444,1111,333,888, etc.
- Causing electronics or lights to flutter or malfunction when you get too close
- The natural desire to seek knowledge and seek the truth

TRIGGERED

A Spiritual Awakening is often triggered by suffering a significant loss or enduring a series of traumatic events.

In many instances, the death of a loved one will trigger a spiritual awakening. Many people try to force or induce an awakening, but a true awakening will only occur when source deems you ready. Meditation, eating healthy and doing online research is great, but I would not recommend seeking unconventional ways to rush the awakening process.

You must first be spiritually cleansed, protected, willing to release fear and raise your vibrations, and having healthy habits, a prayer life or powerful faith are all things that can contribute to raising your vibrations. Seek guidance from a reliable source to ensure random methods that you find online will not be harmful to you.

Having an awakening is tapping into the source, and you will be exposed to many things, some things you may have noticed as a child and some of us have had a sixth sense their entire life.

An actual awakening will eventually bring you a sense of knowing, and confirmation that you will not have to seek validation for your experiences from a single living soul ever again.

I had my spiritual awakening after my Aunt Priscilla passed away. My aunt was a religious woman and was like a mother to me. She was a Baptist minister, and she gave a lot and received a lot. She was blessed and highly favored. Her work was done here on Earth at 63 and she passed away from heart failure. She was tired of the device in her heart and all the ongoing issues. She finally decided for the doctors not to resuscitate after her heart stopped for the final time.

I spoke to her a few hours prior to her passing but did not understand how severe her condition was. I just thought it was another typical visit to the hospital behind her ailing heart issues.

I can imagine it being much harder allowing yourself to transition, knowing and thinking of the pain of the loved ones that were closest to you. We were 800 miles away in Virginia and she was in South Carolina. I guess God could no longer wait for his angel.

I sang at my aunt's funeral, which ended up being standing room only from the floor to the balconies. My aunt was a loved and famed woman who helped everyone. You can imagine the crowds of a hometown hero. I sang for her.

In a series of dreams that came after, she showed me she was in the audience of her own funeral, and also at her own re-pass.

Many people have a false sense of what the awakening process is like. Some think it is all lilies and butterflies, happiness, and hippie life. Well, I will be the first to tell you that you must go through the darkness to get to the light. The first thing we must do is reprogram the fear out of ourselves, that fear is a result of conditioning.

CONDITIONING

It is my belief that everyone is born with spiritual gifts that they have been conditioned to suppress. The conditioning starts with horror films, scary stories, parents/guardians, religion, and government control.

Horror films and scary stories condition us to be afraid. They teach us to fear those bumps in the night, or the mysterious sounds that we cannot explain. Guardians or parents, pacify the young child by telling them that what they are seeing, hearing, or feeling is only in their imagination, for example, the monster in the closet, or their 'imaginary friend.'

Many religions will tell us that having supernatural gifts, or psychic abilities, is demonic or witchcraft.

Last, the government puts fluoride in our water and toothpaste, which calcifies our 'Pineal Gland' or 'Third

Eye," which is a passageway for our extra sensory abilities.

After decades of being afraid, the awakening process showed me I was normal, and it was natural for me to have my gifts. God chose me and the world couldn't turn it off.

MY FIRST ENCOUNTER

At the young age of five, I had my first memorable encounter with a ghostly or spiritual being. Although I had my own room, I would sleep on the bottom bunk bed in my brother's room because I would often hear things that no one could explain. I was scared to sleep in my room alone.

On this night, spirit didn't care if I was alone in my room or not and I was abruptly awakened out of my sleep by loud footsteps on the staircase. Outside of the night-light in the room, all the lights in the house were off and instinctively I knew that whoever or whatever was walking on the stairs was not any of my family members. I laid as still as I could and quietly pulled the covers over my head in fear of seeing anything and anything noticing that I was awake.

The footsteps entered the room.

The entity walked closer and closer to me, and just stood over me.

I could feel its glare piercing through the blanket. I tried my hardest not to breathe because I was so scared. After laying frozen in place for what seemed like forever, the footsteps retreated into the darkness of the stairwell and repeated the cycle on the stairs over, and over, and over.

It was as if it was trapped and stuck in that space. As if it attached a scenario or significant point in its past to that stairway. After what felt like two hours of this dreadfulness, I finally mustered up enough courage and concocted a plan to escape this ghastly entrapment.

I waited for this ghostly being to get back to the bottom of the steps and made a mad dash past the stairway to jump straight into bed with my parents. Startled, my mother asked me what was wrong, I told her exactly what I had just experienced. My mother comforted me and allowed me to attempt to sleep peacefully in the security of my parents' room. Although my mother could not validate what I had experienced, she never made me feel like I was making things up or simply losing it.

In hindsight, I am very grateful to my parents for not sending me back to bed, and just telling me that there's no such thing as the boogie man. I can just imagine how terrifying that would have been to be thrust right back into that scary situation and the residual effects of not having some comfort, support, or relief.

The happenings of that night continued, almost identical in nature, night after night, after night and I could often feel a presence in the home at different points throughout the day for the two years that we were stationed at Shaw Air Force Base, in Sumter, SC.

As a result, I would either find solace in my parents' room or I would lay awake with the covers over my head until I could see a glimmer of light from the rising sun. I always felt safer with the rising of the sun, as if the sunlight was a source of protection.

EIGHT CLAIR SENSES

I n an effort to grasp the velocity of unexplainable phenomenon, many use classifications of the different psychic senses, or the 'Clair' senses.

- Clairvoyance–Is the ability to SEE from the mind's eye (through visions) or your actual physical eyes, which is less common.
- Clairsentience – Is the ability to FEEL things around a situation, person, or experience. This is likely the most common of the 'Clairs.'
- Clairaudience – Is the ability to HEAR in the spiritual realm. You may hear your angels and guides, or past loved ones.
- Claircognizance – Is KNOWING. When you get an answer out of the blue or suddenly

know something without a doubt. This confirmation may come from your higher self, spirit guides, or loved ones that have passed.

- Clairempathy – Is effortlessly picking up on the EMOTIONS of another person, while you are physically around them.
- Clairtangency – Is the sense of psychic TOUCH. By touching an object, one can tell you places the object has been, who has owned it, and more.
- Clairalience – Is clear SMELLING. This is when you smell odors randomly with no physical source for the smell to come from. Someone may smell a full floral burst, a familiar scent or even a horrid dread full stench, out of absolutely nowhere.
- Clairgustance – Is clear TASTING. The ability to taste things you have not eaten.

I bet some of you did not know you had psychic abilities until now. Just think about the occasions where some of the listed happenings occurred for you.

We *all* have gifts and typically you can decide if you want to sharpen your unique abilities or not, and then there are others that have a calling that cannot be denied or ignored.

smoke/steam floating presence, as it moved it left writings on the wall that disappeared. Conduit, tower, radio receiving frequency. Twins, stay rooted.

RED ROOM

Great news guys! I successfully made it out of high school and was starting as a freshman at Virginia State University, in Petersburg, Virginia.

Virginia State University is a HBCU, Historically Black College and University, founded May 6, 1882. There was a lot of history in this place, the buildings and dorms were grand and had a lot of character, but VSU was highly known for being a party school. I chose it for the exceptional Mass Communications programs, not the parties (wink).

Settling into the dorms, I was lucky enough to have my friend Kelly from high school be my roommate. We lived in Howard Hall Dormitory. Virginia State was outstanding from the start, although we noticed a few odd things about our dorm room. The room was warm, although it was still warm outside in August. We noticed that some neighboring rooms were chilled, and their air condition was working fine. Kelly's mom mentioned this to the Resident Assistant who said they would have maintenance check it out. So, we thought nothing of it and settled in.

Kelly and I adopted our next-door neighbor Shayla as our third roomie. She refused to leave our room, but we made space for her all the same. We were enjoying our college experience. We were making great friends, getting good grades, and attending great parties. Thee oh so famous Civic. People would come from far and wide, to little old Petersburg, Virginia, just to party at the Civic.

We were now in the middle of winter and the temperature issues in our room still were not resolved. We complained frequently. The school sent workers and HVAC people to check the system and the vents, but they could not find the issue. Our room was freezing.

What made things so strange is, although we shared the same HVAC system with the neighboring rooms, our room was the only one freezing. The staff seemed to know something more, and they were eager to accommodate us with electric heaters. That would have to suffice until spring.

One night my roomies and I did something different and watched a horror movie for a change. We would normally indulge in comedies or musical plays. Kelly watched 'Bring It On' about 500 times, and we both watched the Tyler Perry Play, 'Diary of a Mad Black Woman" another 500 times. We knew all the words. We had academics, not cable.

Anyway, we watched a horror film and for some odd reason we all can remember everything except the name of this film. I feel that spirit is protecting someone from indulging in it when they probably shouldn't. No need for promoting it. The film was very scary. For it not to be a blockbuster, it sure unlocked something in the room. After watching this movie, a series of events occurred. One right after the other.

The following nights after watching the horror film, I had a series of nightmares. These nightmares were all premonitions of actual events that would soon occur. In the first nightmare I was riding in the backseat of my uncle's new convertible, an old school Cadillac, having a blast and enjoying the breeze. Suddenly my uncle goes faster and faster. Not noticing a teen on his bike trying to cross the street, my uncle breezes past, clipping the boy's tire. Suddenly I feel immense pressure on my neck. I am struggling for air, but neither my uncle nor the passenger notices. I grab around my neck and it feels like an arm, then I feel hands. I am choking, and I can't even make a sound to call for help. The weight of an entire body and the seatbelt keeping me from flying out of the car along with this young man. Suddenly the pressure is immensely lighter and bearable, but the arms and hands are still clenched around my neck. I finally untangled the hands and let out a loud scream as I gasped for the air I was missing.

My uncle finally slows down the car as I realize the young man's body was severed at the waist and he was on the ground behind us in the distance, in pieces. I awoke to the morning news the next day, a student at William and Mary was hit and killed while riding his bike.

The following night I dreamt that I was holding a baby, who appeared to be about 5 months old. The baby would not stop crying and my dear aunt took the baby for a walk around the house. I noticed my aunt going into the bathroom and I followed her to see what her remedy would be to quite the baby. When I turned the corner into the bathroom, I couldn't register the scene fast enough before my aunt flushed the baby down the toilet. I was frozen in shock as the baby popped back up, significantly smaller than she was before.

Before I could grab the baby out of the toilet, my aunt flushed the baby again. The baby popped back up as a little bloody fetus. I jolted out of my sleep, grateful that was only a nightmare. That day one of my dear friends confided in me that she had just returned to school, she had left to get an abortion.

I had a few more nightmares that vaguely predicted deaths or tragic events, unfortunately they were not clear enough for me to warn anyone because the dream would never be about the person the act happened too.

After about five nights of horrid dreams and events, Kelly, Shayla, and I woke up to a very loud banging on the roof. It sounded like a sledgehammer repeatedly.

Bang... bang... banging on the roof.

We got up and asked our neighbors if they heard anything. None of them heard a thing.

Another night I was awakened out of my sleep to see the reflection of what appeared to be hieroglyphics on the dorm room wall. I woke Kelly up so she could see it too; I had to make sure I wasn't losing my mind. The reflection was coming from the streetlight shining through the window, but when I waved my arm in front of the window, the strange script didn't change at all.

I was reduced to turning on the lights and trying to act like I didn't see what I saw.

The last straw was when Kelly, Shayla and I all woke up itching in different areas. Kelly was itching on her thigh, Shayla on her opposite thigh, and I was itching on my breast. We all looked and noticed that we had long scratches on us that had already scabbed up, thus causing the itching. At this point Kelly and I found other friends to crash with as much as possible, and Shayla was forced to retreat to her own room.

One night I was alone in my dorm room, quickly trying to grab some items to leave when the landline phone rang. It was a call from my friend named Fella. Fella was a senior and he knew a lot about the university. I sat on my bed and put my bags down and told fella about all the events we were experiencing in the room. Fella said,

"Are you in Howard Hall?"

"Yes"

"Are you in the room top floor on the far side facing the gym?"

"YES, how do you know that?"

"That is the red room."

"Oh my god, what is the red room?"

"Back in the early 1900s a girl stayed in your same dorm room. The girl was raped and became pregnant. She hid her pregnancy and gave birth in the room. She and the baby both died and there was blood all over the room from her hemorrhaging and bleeding out. The bodies were discovered, removed, and the room was locked up and sealed. When they removed the deadbolts and locks to clean the room, it was spotless as if nothing ever happened. Hence the name Red Room."

I was petrified. I instantly could feel the heaviness and sadness of a ghost that wanted us to know what happened to her. This explained why Kelly, Shayla, and I all had scratches in intimate areas on our bodies.

I asked the manager of our dorm about the story and she said it was just a rumor. In all actuality, I am sure it was a coverup. It's hard to market a haunted dormitory.

REPROGRAMING

As stated previously the first thing that one must achieve is the release of fear. Fear will hinder the spiritual connection and may invite wrong entities into your space. The spirit realm operates off energy and vibrations.

Evil energies will vibrate very low, good energies will operate off very high vibrations. Our goal is to keep our vibrations as high as possible as much as possible.

You want to channel everything that is good.

Ask for the protection and the guidance of your ancestors, your guides, God, angels, whatever is suitable for you to feel secure and elevated. I suggest regular prayer and meditation, and that you ask for guidance from the spirit realm and the source before exploring or venturing into the layers of the spirit realm. Always be mindful that once the door is opened, it is up to you what comes through it.

Beware of False Prophets.

False prophets will come to you as a family member, friend, mate, associate, co-worker and sometimes even a pastor or stranger. They will tell you what you cannot do, what relationship will not work, what house you cannot buy, what career you won't ever get. Realize some of those people are speaking to their own abilities, not yours. Some of those people have ill intent, and they want to deter you from your path. Listen to yourself because you will know when these people are around you. Do not ignore this, do not ignore yourself. Ignoring the truth from within is equivalent to ignoring God.

Pray for Discernment.

Ask for a stronger connection to the source so that you can hear the word clearly. Once you have achieved that direct connection you will not have to look outside of yourself for the answers that you seek.

ANGELS AND SPIRITS

We have a team of master souls assigned to help us learn what we need to gain from our earthly experience. Consider earth a school for our souls. Notice the trials and errors, ups and downs, joys, and pains etc.

What we gain from this life determines if we have lived in our purpose and learned the intended lessons. Once we have mastered our lessons our soul can stop cycling back to earth (reincarnation) and we can reside in the higher dimensions, and/or work as spirit guides.

Spirit guides were once human, they have mastered their lessons and are also regarded as Ascended Masters.

Angels are immortal celestial beings of light who only exist to serve the Divine Source, and work between the divine realms and human realms.

Angels are not and never have been human. Encounters are rare and often beyond human perception. An Angel can take many forms but will appear to us as a male or female so that we can understand, but they are genderless. A Guardian Angel is assigned to a soul, resides with it before conception, through birth and through life.

Angels and spirits work together to guide and protect us through our journey. In many circumstances we must ask for guidance and assistance to ensure we have learned something before the guides intervene. So they do not intervene too soon, you are acknowledging their presence, and you learned the intended lesson in order for you to ask them for guidance.

THOUGHTS AND DREAMS...

_____

_____

_____

_____

_____

_____

_____

_____

EARTH ANGEL

Things were fairly normal for a while, then at sixteen, I attended my school prom with my friend Zo and we went with a group of his friends and their dates. We all left prom together and attended an after party. Then we went to eat at IHOP. It was around 2 am, four cars of teens zooming down the highway.

I was riding in the car with Zo, and his friend Trey was riding alone in the car behind us. Suddenly the cars sped up to race. The cars started going faster, and faster, and faster. I was very nervous and asked Zo to slow down. Zo would not listen. So, I told Zo to slow down because the police frequent this street, and its prom night!

As soon as Zo heard me mention the police, he slowed down to a normal speed, unfortunately Trey was not paying attention and had to cut his wheel to avoid a collision with us. He slammed into a pole head-on at a very high speed.

Although we were not prom dates, Trey and I were very close friends. Him being dead or severely injured in this mangled car was too much to fathom.

Zo turned his car around, we pulled up to the crash and Zo ran up to Trey's car, I on the other hand inched toward the car slowly, in fear of what I was about to see. In hindsight, I was on the verge of a full-on panic attack. There was no flowing traffic, and no one around to help.

Then, a man appeared out of nowhere and said, "He's going to be all right."

Strangely, those few words from this stranger gave me complete peace. I turned for a split second to look at the crash scene; I looked back for the nice man, but he had vanished. I didn't have time to think much about it at that moment, but it was very odd because there were no other cars, homes, or anything close enough for him to retreat to and be gone in a split second.

I turned, went up to the wreck. The pole had crushed the front driver's side and Trey was saved by inches. Trey was bleeding and something trapped his lower body inside the mangled vehicle. I was able to assist him and get something to stop the bleeding, all due to the calming words of a stranger.

The authorities arrived, Trey was cut from the vehicle, and rushed to the hospital. Some broken bones and scratches. But as the stranger said, Trey came out all right.

At a later date, I discussed what I saw with Trey. I told him how the man appeared out of nowhere. The man was white with thick black hair and a black mustache. He had on a red construction plaid shirt, blue jeans, and black leather construction boots. When the man spoke to me, his lips never moved, it was like, telepathy. He spoke clearly, without speaking at all, but I was calmed in an instant. He gave me a peace that was effortless, and hard to explain.

I knew I had seen an angel.

SOUTHERN HOSPITALITY

As kids, my brother and I would go visit my father's side of the family in Beaufort, SC every summer. A few of those summers we were tasked with babysitting our younger twin cousins.

On a typical day, the twins would partly behave and listen to us, UNTIL aunt Priscilla came home. When my auntie was around the twins would act completely different, and just be outright bad as if they were holding the badness in all day until my aunt came home.

Well, my brother, being the trickster that he is, came up with his own retaliation for the twin's troublesome behavior.

PRANKS.

While laying down half asleep in the room that Ashley and I shared, My brother called me into the room he shared with Ian and when I entered he looked at me with laughter in his eyes and said watch this, my brother stood Ian up straight, although Ian was deep asleep, and we would watch him half way try to stand and catch him right before he could tumble over onto the floor because he was still asleep.

As teenagers, this was hilarious to watch. Just playful pranks. The pranks would continue, but only on the days that the twins misbehaved the worst.

One night my brother woke me up with pranking on his mind. My brother came into my room, turned the light on and closed the door, spray bottle in hand, fully ready to prank little Ashley. Suddenly, we heard heavy footsteps coming from the far end of the hallway where my aunt and uncle slept. Instinctively, my brother turned off my light and hopped in the bed, atop of the covers to the left side of me and faked like he was asleep.

We lay there, still, me in the middle laying on my back, Ashley to my right fast asleep and my brother to my left. These were slow dragging steps, unlike that of my aunt and uncle who would have moved faster, especially if they thought we may have been up to mischief.

My brother and I heard the steps coming closer and closer until finally, the steps were in the room. I think both my brother and I simultaneously realized that there was CLEARLY someone in the room walking slowly around the bed from one side to the other, yet, the bedroom door never opened. So how would they have gotten in the room?

We lay there paralyzed with fear.

Our eyes shut tight and we tried to relax and appear as sleep as one could look. The footsteps dragged along the carpet loudly, from one side of the bed to the other, as if to analyze and observe us. I did not understand what this thing' was looking for, but I knew for certain I didn't want to find out. The entity lingered in the room, just walking about freely. We wouldn't dare look, but we could hear every step.

In an effort to wake Ashley up, without being detected, I pinched her arm. Ashley did not budge. I pinched Ashley's arm harder; I was certain this would wake her; she still did not move. I pinched Ashley's arm again, and almost as if she was in a trance, Ashley didn't move a muscle. This was unreal.

We continued to lay there, not moving a muscle, until, through our shut eyelids, we could detect light in the room. I took the slightest peek and could see that it was now dawn.

Tired of being paralyzed in fear, and gaining a little extra courage from the daylight, I yelled to the top of my lungs, AUNT CILLAAA- UNCLE HERMAN LEEEEEE…

I heard a scurry to our room, and my aunt appeared and asked what was wrong and why LJ was in the room. We told her what happened, what we heard, how the thing had walked through the door. We told her everything. My aunt blamed what we heard on a leaky faucet in the bathroom next door. Both my brother and I knew what we heard, and we knew that it had nothing to do with dripping water.

For me, being someone that can see, hear, and feel spirits, there was nothing more gratifying than my older brother sharing that experience with me. He was frightened, but it was all too refreshing to finally have a skeptic validate my claims with such enthusiasm.

Until this day my brother will tell that story with the same precise detail, as he did over twenty years ago.

MEDITATION AND PRAYER

I t is always great to pray, but many people do not pray effectively. Meditation is a way to dive deep within one's inner self, access your higher self, set intentions, express gratitude, ask for guidance, all while shifting into a heightened state of mind.

Meditation requires you to be relaxed and comfortable, but not in full sleep mode. There is a balance of emptying the mind and controlled breathing to put you in a meditative state.

I find it very effective to meditate to Binaural Beats, or even guided meditation may help you get started. Meditation is one of the most effective ways to understand and soothe yourself through the awakening process.

THOUGHTS AND DREAMS...

_____

_____

_____

_____

_____

_____

_____

_____

SOUND HEALING

Sound healing uses vibrations or vocal instruments, like gongs, Tibetan singing bowls, and tuning forks, to relax your mind and body. Different frequencies are known to have different soothing effects.

Binaural beats use many of these ancient healing sounds and frequencies, and I find them to be very effective with relaxation and meditation. Binaural beats are easy to access on popular music apps like iTunes and YouTube.

You may also find guided meditation helpful.

SMUDGING

Most commonly known as burning sage, smudging is one way to cleanse a space and invite positive energy.

When smudging you burn plant material like sage, sweetgrass, lavender, lemongrass, rosemary, and Palo Santo. You may acquire sage bundles with a mixture of different sacred herbs. Sage bundles and other smudging herbs can be found at your local spiritual store, and online retailers.

- Be sure to check reviews and research your source to ensure you are getting the real thing.
- Be sure to have windows or doors opened, then light the smudging stick until the smoke is continuous.

- Push the smoke throughout the entire home.
- Do not forget closets, bathrooms, and basements when cleansing your home.

I personally like to deep clean my home prior to smudging, but I also smudge in between deep cleanings.

YOGA

Yoga is an ancient system of physical and mental practices that originated during the Indus Valley civilization in South Asia. The fundamental purpose of yoga is to foster harmony in the body, mind, and environment. Yoga professes a complete system of physical, mental, social, and spiritual development. Yoga is a systematic practice of physical exercise, breath control, relaxation, diet control, and positive thinking and meditation aimed at developing harmony in the body, mind, and environment.

The practice entails low-impact physical activity, postures (called asanas), breathing techniques (pranayama), relaxation, and meditation.

Most people are familiar with the physical poses or

yoga positions but don't know that yoga involves so much more.

CRYSTALS AND STONES

Healing crystals contain the life-giving elements of the Earth and the universe. The stones harness the energy of the sun and moon with unique attributions and distinct healing qualities. We have used healing crystals since the beginning of time. The stones can help you raise your vibration and be more aligned with the universe when used properly and with intent. Crystals may be pretty to look at but do also hold much power. Here is a list of 20 healing crystals and their attributes.

- Selenite: The Master
- Moonstone: The Stabilizer
- Aventurine: The Stone of Opportunity
- Crystal Quartz: The Spirit Stone

- Citrine: The Money Stone
- Agate: Stone of Inner Stability
- Tourmaline: The Grounding Stone
- Rose Quartz: The Love Stone
- Turquoise: The Stone of Protection
- Fluorite: The Stone of Positivity
- Lapis Lazuli: The Stone of Truth
- Hematite: The Grounding Stone
- Jade: The Dream Stone
- Amethyst: The Manifestation Stone
- Kyanite: The Stone of Emotion
- Obsidian: The Mirror Stone
- Blue Topaz: The Stone of Creativity
- Opal: The Eye Stone
- ▪Amazonite: Stone of Courage
- Garnet: The Stone of Health and Creativity

I've included the following crystal/mineral resource for you as well:

HOWLITE
Can eliminate rage and calm violent, uncontrolled anger. Believed good for teeth and bones.

JASPER
Said to be useful for controlling the emotions and a good stone for soothing the nerves.

LABRADORITE
A blazing, fire-like stone said to protect and cushion one's aura, as well as providing wisdom and understanding.

LAPIS LAZULI
Considered to be the 'stone of friendship'. It is said to protect one from physical danger and encourage honesty and dignity.

MALACHITE
Known as the 'stone of transformation', assisting one in times of change. It is reputed to benefit sufferers of shyness.

MOONSTONE
A feminine stone, inspiring flexibility, nurturing and wisdom and believed helpful in pregnancy.

SERPENTINE (NEW JADE)
A mysterious stone thought to enhance the emotions of love and assist in meditation.

ORANGE CALCITE
Soft, tranquil, happy and healthy, this stone is all of these and more. It is said to aid the acquisition of wisdom.

QUARTZ
Is used as a tool for therapy and acts as an excellent channeller for healing. Believed good for the brain and soul by dispelling negativity.

RHODONITE
A stimulating stone thought good for dispelling anxiety, encouraging generosity and providing a general feeling of well-being.

ROSE QUARTZ
Known as the 'love stone'. Aids peacefulness and calm in relationships. Said to ease stress and tension and assist sleep.

RUTILATED QUARTZ
This stone is thought to improve the mood and open one's aura. The delicate encapsulated rutiles deepen the powers of the quartz crystal.

SNOWFLAKE OBSIDIAN
A 'stone of purity' bringing balance to the body, mind and spirit. Said to be beneficial for the skin and veins.

SODALITE
Helps to calm and clear the mind, bring joy and relieve a heavy heart. Said to aid the metabolism and lymphatic system.

TIGER EYE
The "confidence stone"- inspires brave but sensible behaviour. Believed to aid the entire digestive system.

TURQURENITE
A form of Magnesite. It can be used to stimulate passion and heart-felt love. Said to aid the treatment of fevers and chills.

TURRITELLA AGATE
Is believed to help in times of change, dispelling negative thoughts and relieving conditions of fatigue.

THOUGHTS AND DREAMS...

_____

_____

_____

_____

_____

_____

_____

THE ROUGH SIDE

The awakening process is not all fun and frills. You will have hard times, long nights, and scary events.

Once the spiritual door is opened, spirit knows that you are now engaged. Many spirits may try to come through to get messages through to others, or be heard from someone in the realm they are most familiar with, thus the random waking times.

To the spirit realm, there is absolutely no such thing as time. You will be jolted out of your sleep by loud noises, whispers, crashes, smashes, or even subtle things that you don't even notice. It will typically occur between three and four in the morning.

This would be a great time to meditate or pray for direction because at this point spirit is trying to communicate with you. This communication could be something that could help direct your immediate steps. These waking occurrences may be overwhelming to those of us that have to work regular jobs, tend to children, or do day-to-day tasks that we have to be up and alert for that day.

I would suggest that you pray for balance and communicate with your guides. Let spirit know what you must deal with on a day-to-day basis, and how the waking times are a hindrance to you. Speak and you will be heard. Eventually the nightly interruptions will subside unless the communication is necessary for your good.

During the rough side you may also feel shortness of breath, anxiety, and quickening of the heartbeat. Not only is your mind going through, but your body will physically go through changes. You may jolt up in the middle of sleep attempting to catch your breath. I believe this is symbolic of you dying in the flesh and coming alive in the spirit. This can happen many nights while going through the awakening experience.

Do not fear.

So long as your lifestyle does not encourage a health issue, you can attribute it to your awakening process. If you have serious concerns, seek medical attention.

Migraines and headaches will occur as physical side effects of your pineal gland coming back to life or decalcifying. You may feel sharp pain in the middle of your forehead slightly above your eye level, also you will feel vibrations in this area. These are signs of your third eye opening.

Vibrations will occur as a physical side effect. We are all composed of vibrations and energy. Bad or evil will have very low vibrations, pleasant or good will have very high vibrations. You may feel uncontrollable vibrations between your eyes, along your spine, and sometimes all over your entire body. This usually occurs when there is a major shift in your energy, or when your soul is leaving or returning from Astral Travel.

Electronics or lights may flutter, malfunction, or fail in your presence. This is not uncommon during enlightenment and even after you have awakened. This phenomenon could result from the elevated levels of energy you now possess and can also be spirit attempting to communicate with you.

Fear can easily consume you, so you must release your fear. Rest assured that nothing can harm you and your angels are protecting you. Most times you can speak out and ask the spirit to stop manipulating the technology and that you are aware they are with you. Sometimes acknowledgment is all spirit wants. I recommend effective meditation and prayer to ask for direction and to give spirit a time when your mind is quieted to deliver the messages they may want to communicate.

Songs on the radio, signs in the media, and even messages from people around you will seem far too coincidental. Keep in mind that there is no such thing as a coincidence. That song on the radio was a message or an answer to your question. That random conversation was confirmation. That commercial or social media post just answered your immediate question. Pay attention to the things going on around you. These are signs and answers.

AFTER THE ROUGH SIDE

fter and during the rough side, you will have the emphatic desire to be in nature. You may want to get in some water, take a hike, camp, take a walk, travel outside of the country, take nature trips, or just sit outdoors. You will feel a heightened connection to nature, trees, and animals. The singing of the birds will be far more relevant. You will have more appreciation for life.

Once enlightenment is reached, things will start lining up according to your thoughts.

On the busiest night of the week, if you think "I am going to pull up to this club and get a parking space right in the front," that parking space will be there for you.

If you want someone to contact you, or think of you, you can think about it and you will get a phone call right after, this is telepathy. A lot of the obstacles and hardships in your life will dissolve into an afterthought.

Your mental health and self-control will elevate to new heights. You will develop a calmness that you never had before and your reaction to things will be better. You will have more self-control.

I learned that we have so much more control and power than we know.

We must simply tap into the Source.

There are many gifts to enlightenment, many advantages, and many magical things you will have the ability to encounter. After I became enlightened, my life became easier. I became a homeowner; I made myself open to love; I am able to handle and react to conflict with ease, and I am more relaxed.

Quieting the mind to let spirit guide me, I fulfilled many of my own personal accomplishments to include becoming an author and starting businesses. Manifesting my desires on a day-to-day basis with guidance from Source.

LUCID DREAMS

One of the many things that you may encounter during and after the awakening process is lucid dreaming. A lucid dream is a dream in which the dreamer is aware that they are dreaming, and they may have some control over the dream. You will be able to make conscious decisions in lucid dreams, and you may also recognize thoughts and emotions.

In a lucid dream you will be able to change the characters, narrative and even the environment.

According to Healthline Media, "About 55 percent of people have experienced one or more lucid dreams in their lifetime, however frequent lucid dreaming is rare. Only 23 percent of people have lucid dreams at least once a month."

Lucid dreaming usually occurs during REM sleep, "Rapid Eye Movement" stage of sleep. By extending the REM stage of sleep you have a better chance of experiencing lucid dreaming. When you practice healthy sleep habits your body can flow through all four stages of sleep.

Ways to improve your sleep patterns and potentially lucid dream:

- Follow a sleep schedule
- Exercise daily
- Avoid electronics before bed
- Create a relaxing environment
- Avoid caffeine and alcohol before bed
- Pray and meditate
- Set the intention to lucid dream
- Ask your spirit guides to help your lucid dream

During the stages of enlightenment, dreams will be very important. You may experience or remember more dreams than usual, have visits from deceased loved ones, and you may receive messages in your dreams.

I highly recommend that you keep a dream journal and write down your dreams right after you have them. Writing down your dreams will help you decipher messages from spirit, it may soothe the rough side of the enlightenment journey, and it will help your brain get accustomed to retaining your dream details.

Reality testing is good to practice during a dream to encourage lucid dreaming.

Popular reality checks according to Healthline include:

- Finger through palm. Push your fingers against your opposite palm. If they pass through, you are dreaming.
- Mirrors. In a dream state, your reflection won't look normal.
- Nose pinch. Pinch your nose. You'll be able to breathe if you're in a dream.
- Reading. Look away from text then look back again. If you're dreaming, the text will change.
- Tattoos. If you have tattoos, look at them. They'll look different in a dream.

According to Healthline, here are some ways to induce lucid dreaming:

Wake back to bed. Set an alarm and wake up five hours after bedtime, you will probably enter the REM stage of sleep while you are still conscious.

Mnemonic induction of lucid dreams (MILD). Tell yourself that you will practice lucid dreaming tonight. You can do it before bed or when you're awake during WBTB.

Wake-initiated lucid dream (WILD). In WILD, you enter REM sleep from wakefulness while maintaining your consciousness. It involves lying down until you have a hypnagogic hallucination.

THOUGHTS AND DREAMS...

_____

_____

_____

_____

_____

_____

_____

ASTRAL PROJECTION

Astral projection (or astral travel) is a term used in esotericism to describe an intentional out-of-body experience (OBE) that assumes the existence of a soul or consciousness called an "astral body" that is separate from the physical body and capable of traveling outside the body and throughout the universe.

Astral Projection is an out-of-body experience that you are conscious of from beginning to end. When and if you ever have this experience, you will be aware of it from before your soul exits the body till you awake. You may not be aware of the re-entry to the physical body, but you will know the feeling of when the soul leaves the body. This is where we have to release all fear because this will feel like death.

You will be semi awake and actually feel your soul leavening your physical body. As I was, many will be frightened of the unknown and naturally will their spirit to return to their body, but some will release that fear and fly along to wherever their soul desires.

I was practicing and doing meditations to induce an Astral Projection experience but for the first few days, nothing happened. Three days later without effort, I awoke to heavy vibrations on my body and face. I opened my eyes and noticed a blue tint on the walls and ceiling of my bedroom. Unclear of what was happening to me, I swung my legs off the side of the bed and sat on the edge of it. Trying to wake fully, I looked around the room and something caught my eye. I was sitting on the edge of the bed fully aware of my position, then I looked to my right and noticed that my legs were still curled up in the fetal position as if I was still laying down sleeping. Too afraid to look to the left of me, I knew that I had successfully Astral Projected.

I was terrified and immediately willed myself to return to my flesh. This occurred without effort on several other occasions. I did fight it out of fear the first few times, but I eventually released that fear and invited Astral Travel into my life.

The extent of the adventures is unexplainable. At a

master level you can control when and where you travel, but for me I was going with the flow of adventure. It is a marvelous and out of this world experience.

SOUL MATE VS. TWIN FLAME

A soulmate is someone you had a past life connection with. It is highly likely that you will encounter multiple soulmates in this lifetime. The soul connection will not always be a romantic one, although many hope to find their soulmate in a love match.

Have you ever seen a stranger but felt a powerful connection to them as if you already knew them?

That could likely be someone from your soul tribe, or someone you knew from a past lifetime. The vibrational frequency will bring soulmates together but we must live in the present and quiet the mind, so we do not miss the pertinent moments, subtle signs from the universe, and confirmation that we are on the right path.

When you encounter your soul mate, you will feel a

magnificent feeling, a God feeling, and when you lock eyes, you know that you are connected.

A twin flame was one energy source at some point, containing a divine masculine energy and a divine feminine energy. That one source divided into two to enter this lifetime. Twin flames think alike, utilize telepathy, and will have a divine similar purpose. There will be a powerful sense of knowing and the feeling of an immensely deep connection.

You may experience heart palpitations, nervousness, or jitters when you come into proximity with your twin flame. This is your heart chakra being activated or opened. Twin flames will have intense, out of this world sex, and develop an unconditional love that can sometimes be overwhelming.

One twin may not initially be receptive to the other, and they will probably run. This resistance is because of a prior relationship, childhood trauma, already being in a relationship or other things that they need to heal from. The desire to run typically occurs from the fear of the tremendous connection, or undefined feelings that the runner twin may not yet recognize. Angels and spirit guides will be working overtime to bring the two together.

Twin flames mirror each other and may share some

similar physical characteristics. The two will have a lot in common, and often there may be friction.

Imagine seeing many of your own flaws mirrored to you from someone else. For twin flames to stay together, they must have a certain level of awakening or be on the same spiritual vibration. Because of programming and conditioning of today's society twin flames could operate on different vibrational frequencies.

Being conscious of this could make your chances of connecting with your twin flame stronger.

Self-love must be practiced for both parties individually, so when twin flames come together, they may both be and feel whole. When twin flames unite, they accomplish exceptional things, and this is what you call a power couple. Both twins aligned in their awakening will make a successful and powerful union.

SOUL TIES

A Soul tie is ultimately an invisible connection that binds two people together and will often lead you to be receptive to manipulation. In most cases we create negative soul ties out of rebellion and a lack of discernment. To rebel against your higher self, and the advice of loved ones, mentors and advisors are usually how soul ties are created.

Learn to view every encounter as a spiritual encounter so you do not confuse a person's mind for their soul state, or who they want to be, versus who they actually are. Soul ties can apply to all types of relationships that you may have, not just romantic relationships and soul ties aren't always negative. When a relationship is draining and heavy and all of your senses advises you to leave the situation, yet you feel bound to that person.

This is a soul tie.

That friend that tries to damage your relationships with others, or that family member that tries to use you or always needs financial help, that spouse that does not want you to grow and wants to control your every move. There are so many relatable situations that would describe a soul tie.

Relationships can have good and bad soul ties, and it is understandable that not every situation is one that you can just walk away from.

Signs of a negative soul tie would have you feeling controlled, manipulated, and obligated to give or do things you do not want to do. Obsessively wanting to pursue a connection with someone who has expressed that they do not want any form of relationship with you or justifying someone else's controlling behavior and having an unhealthy dependency on them are all examples of negative soul ties.

When you break negative soul ties many negative cycles in your life will end. Breaking soul ties begins with identifying that they exist. Next you must forgive the person or circumstances that caused the hurt so you can take back your power.

Some may seek prayer from a prayer group, meditate, or set the intention and ask your angels and guides to help you break those non- serving connections. You can take a spiritual journey, travel in nature, exercise, also practice and create new positive habits.

Changing your lifestyle may naturally make you unavailable and remove you from the soul connections.

CHAKRAS

Chakras are the 7 energy centers of the body, starting from the base of your spine going up to the crown of your head. Evidence of Chakras date back to 1400 B.C. and are believed to originate in India.

We have more than 7 Chakras but the main 7 are what we will discuss. Each Chakra corresponds with a different organ in your body and facilitates with your emotional, spiritual, and psychological position.

Your Chakras can be balanced, blocked, or overactive.

On the next page is a guide from www.thewordisallyours.com that you may find helpful.

THE 7 MAIN CHAKRAS

ROOT
RED
SURVIVAL, GROUNDING

LOCATION: TAIL BONE
INCENSE: VETIVER
CRYSTAL: RED GARNET
ESSENTIAL OIL: CEDARWOOD

SACRAL
ORANGE
SEXUALITY, PASSION

LOCATION: NAVEL
INCENSE: PATCHOULI
CRYSTAL: CARNELIAN
ESSENTIAL OIL: YLANG YLANG

SOLAR PLEXUS
YELLOW
CONFIDENCE, INTUITION

LOCATION: SOLAR PLEXUS
INCENSE: GERANIUM
CRYSTAL: CITRINE
ESSENTIAL OIL: CINNAMON

HEART
GREEN
LOVE, COMPASSION

LOCATION: CHEST
INCENSE: ROSE
CRYSTAL: EMERALD
ESSENTIAL OIL: ROSE

THROAT
BLUE
EXPRESSION, CREATIVITY

LOCATION: THROAT
INCENSE: SANDALWOOD
CRYSTAL: SODALITE
ESSENTIAL OIL: EUCALYPTUS

THIRD EYE
INDIGO
PSYCHIC ABILITY

LOCATION: FOREHEAD
INCENSE: JASMINE
CRYSTAL: LABRADORITE
ESSENTIAL OIL: LAVENDER

CROWN
VIOLET
CONNECTION, WISDOM

LOCATION: ABOVE HEAD
INCENSE: FRANKINCENSE
CRYSTAL: AMETHYST
ESSENTIAL OIL: MYRHH

WWW.THEWORLDISALLYOURS.COM

LISTED HERE ARE 7 Chakras and information on each, and a yoga pose or ways to balance the Chakra:

Crown Chakra

(Top of the head, Color~ Purple: Associated with consciousness):

- Balanced: Bliss, faith, connection with spirit, spirituality, self-actualization, universal love, awareness, understanding, wisdom
- Overactive: Obsessiveness, being critical, spiritual addiction, isolation
- Blocked: Ungrounded, depression, anxiety, learning disabilities, mental block, earth attachment
- Head stand

Third Eye Chakra

(Forehead in between your eyebrows, Color~ Indigo):

- Balanced: Intuition, manifestation, psychic abilities, visions or communication in the spiritual realm, spiritual awareness, clarity

- Overactive: Nightmares, fearfulness, delusions, obsessiveness
- Blocked: Poor imagination, not feeling connected to spirit or source, cannot listen to your inner thoughts
- Downward dog, dream journal, being under the stars

Throat Chakra

(Throat area, Color~ Blue):

- Balanced: Clear communication, confidence, great expression, transparency, good listening abilities, leadership abilities
- Blocked: Arguing, being misunderstood secrets, not communicating, not being a good listener
- Overactive: Loud, using harsh words, opinionated, argumentative, gossip
- Shoulder Stand, Journal

Heart Chakra

(Chakra of love, Color~ Green):

- Balanced: Compassion, love, tolerance, peace, forgiveness, gratitude, having meaningful relationships
- Blocked: Grief, Bitter, hateful, trust issues, issues with connections and relationships
- Overactive: Over attachment, over apologizing, co-dependent, giving too much, obsessiveness resulting in jealousy
- Camel pose, Being in nature and around animals

Solar Plexus Chakra

(Middle of Body, Color~Yellow)

- Balanced: Drive confidence, great self-esteem, will power, assertiveness, wisdom
- Overactive: Domineering, perfectionist, power hungry, judgmental, critical control issues
- Blocked: Low self-esteem, powerless, submissive, shame, victim mentality
- Warrior Pose

Sacral Chakra

(Below your navel, Color~ Orange)

- Balanced: Joy, pleasure, sensuality, procreation, passion, sexuality, optimism
- Overactive: Over emotional, sex addicts, manipulative, self-fulfillment
- Blocked: Low sex drive, fear of intimacy, isolation, guilt
- Yoga Pose, Goddess Pose, go in the moon light, dancing

Root Chakra

(Base of the spine, Color~ Red)

- Balanced: Safe, secure, centered, grounded, happy, survival
- Overactive: Materialistic, greedy, money hungry
- Blocked: Instability, financial issues, anxiety, fear
- Ground, barefoot on the earth, gardening, Yoga Tree Pose

THERE ARE distinct ways to balance your chakras, some use dance, yoga, meditation, music, singing, painting, prayer, whatever makes you feel good.

In addition, spiritual cleanses, spiritual baths, acupuncture. Crystal work is a huge way that many people balance their Chakras.

Allow yourself to open up to self-healing and you will feel the change when balance is achieved.

Whatever method you use, you must also set the intention of what you want to accomplish.

THOUGHTS AND DREAMS...

_____

_____

_____

_____

_____

_____

_____

DISCOVERY OF A LIFETIME

AN ESSAY WRITTEN FOR MY FIRST ENGLISH COLLEGE ASSIGNMENT AT THE AGE OF 17

My discovery did not need much research or observation. This feeling is something that some people experience throughout their lifetime, but unfortunately some never experience it at all. It is also one of the most complicated things in the world.

My discovery is LOVE.

This love is not your typical love. I am speaking love on a whole new level. Not love from your boyfriend or girlfriend, not love for your brand-new car or material things, not love that fluctuates from sometimes I do, and sometimes I don't.

This is love on a whole new level.

This kind of love makes you feel so good inside, like you have never felt before. It's better than anything you could ever imagine. It is better than the best sex you have ever had, it will get you higher than the most expensive drug around, and it can relieve you of all your worries and stresses.

Best of all, this love is unconditional and everlasting. There is truly no other love like this.

I am speaking about the love of God.

Many people say, "Yeah, yeah, yeah, I hear this all the time. You have to be all holy to get that feeling, and I have done too many bad things in my life."

You are wrong if you feel this way.

This feeling usually overcomes people when they are at their lowest point and I am a prime example. I have seen some things in my seventeen years that I truly regret. When I encountered this overwhelming experience, I was skipping school from time to time and I was a little depressed. I thought I was having a good time, and I was not looking to change.

My mother and I went to visit my aunt Inez at her church in Norfolk, Virginia, and that is where I first got that wonderful feeling. Again, many people think church is boring, or they will just fall asleep, this is because they have not been to the right church, delivering the right message. I was at the right place at the right time and everything was right. The preacher spoke a glorious sermon, and it seemed like he was speaking directly to me. I was so moved by his approach and delivery that I wanted him to go on, and on, and on. I never cry in front of others, but I felt no shame on that day. I could not control the tears.

A feeling of joy, peace, hope and love was so overwhelming that I do not think anyone could have contained their reaction. I felt refreshed, like a new person. It was as if I had a brand-new chance. Any doubts I had before about people shouting or fainting in church were gone. I now knew the power of God, and I wanted to know him better.

After I experienced this discovery of a lifetime, I wanted everyone I knew and cherished to feel it. That is just how great it is. This kind of love could make anyone do a complete turnaround, a serious three-sixty. I have also recognized that some of the best preachers and ministers have been through a lot, and some have even been to jail. Their delivery methods are so successful because they have sat on the bad side of the table too. They have the advantage of seeing things from both points of view and not just one-sided.

You can have that love in your heart, and yet there will be many times when you slip up, but that is merely because we are human.

Today I am not perfect, and I still make many mistakes, but I am working on all my faults and I know that the lord knows my heart. God is truly my support system and my solid rock; without God I would have crumbled a long time ago.

When and if you ever feel this love, you will definitely know, and I hope you remember this article and the girl who tried to describe her discovery of a lifetime the best way she knew how.

FULL CIRCLE

I have detailed only a few of my supernatural experiences, and most of them frightened me miserably. As I went through life, I realized that I could make others see, or have the sensitivity to hear ghosts or spirits even if they've never had an experience before.

My awakening was necessary because now I understand what I was going through and I further understand that fear only feeds the negative. Sometimes spirit just wants to be acknowledged.

Once spirit knows that you have that 6th sense they will often work overtime and tell their spirit friends about you and bombard you at all times of the night, wanting to communicate or get messages to loved ones. This would usually occur to me through dreams.

If this is happening to you and becomes overwhelming, focus on your third eye chakra, and make sure it is not overactive. Practice balancing your third eye chakra.

THOUGHTS AND DREAMS...

OUTRO

My book lists a small portion of the immense vastness of the great awakening experience. Everyone's journey will have similarities and differences.

This is a guide, a tool, and a resource to help you understand and grow spiritually.

Always remember LOVE is the highest vibration.

Peace and Blessings and thank you for reading my book.

PEACE, LOVE, and LIGHT.

THOUGHTS AND DREAMS...

THOUGHTS AND DREAMS...

_____

_____

_____

_____

_____

_____

_____

THOUGHTS AND DREAMS...

_____

_____

_____

_____

_____

_____

_____

_____

THOUGHTS AND DREAMS...

_____

_____

_____

_____

_____

_____

_____

THOUGHTS AND DREAMS...

THOUGHTS AND DREAMS...

_____

_____

_____

_____

_____

_____

_____

_____

THOUGHTS AND DREAMS...

_____

_____

_____

_____

_____

_____

_____

THOUGHTS AND DREAMS...

_____

_____

_____

_____

_____

_____

_____

_____

THOUGHTS AND DREAMS...

_____

_____

_____

_____

_____

_____

_____

_____

THOUGHTS AND DREAMS...

_____

_____

_____

_____

_____

_____

_____

THOUGHTS AND DREAMS...

THOUGHTS AND DREAMS...

_____

_____

_____

_____

_____

_____

_____

THOUGHTS AND DREAMS...

_____

_____

_____

_____

_____

_____

_____

THOUGHTS AND DREAMS...

_____

_____

_____

_____

_____

_____

_____

THOUGHTS AND DREAMS...

_____

_____

_____

_____

_____

_____

_____

THOUGHTS AND DREAMS...

THOUGHTS AND DREAMS...

_____

_____

_____

_____

_____

_____

_____

_____

THOUGHTS AND DREAMS...

_____

_____

_____

_____

_____

_____

_____

THOUGHTS AND DREAMS...

THOUGHTS AND DREAMS...

_____

_____

_____

_____

_____

_____

_____

THOUGHTS AND DREAMS...

_____

_____

_____

_____

_____

_____

_____

_____

THOUGHTS AND DREAMS...

_____

_____

_____

_____

_____

_____

_____

THOUGHTS AND DREAMS...

THOUGHTS AND DREAMS...

_____

_____

_____

_____

_____

_____

_____

THOUGHTS AND DREAMS...

_____

_____

_____

_____

_____

_____

_____

THOUGHTS AND DREAMS...

_____

_____

_____

_____

_____

_____

_____

_____

THOUGHTS AND DREAMS...

THOUGHTS AND DREAMS...

THOUGHTS AND DREAMS...

THOUGHTS AND DREAMS...

_____

_____

_____

_____

_____

_____

_____

THOUGHTS AND DREAMS...

_____

_____

_____

_____

_____

_____

_____

_____

THOUGHTS AND DREAMS...

_____

_____

_____

_____

_____

_____

_____

THOUGHTS AND DREAMS...

_____

_____

_____

_____

_____

_____

_____

_____

THOUGHTS AND DREAMS...

_____

_____

_____

_____

_____

_____

_____

THOUGHTS AND DREAMS...

_____

_____

_____

_____

_____

_____

_____

_____

THOUGHTS AND DREAMS...

_____

_____

_____

_____

_____

_____

_____

THOUGHTS AND DREAMS...

_____

_____

_____

_____

_____

_____

_____

THOUGHTS AND DREAMS...

_____

_____

_____

_____

_____

_____

_____

_____

THOUGHTS AND DREAMS...

_____

_____

_____

_____

_____

_____

_____

THOUGHTS AND DREAMS...

THOUGHTS AND DREAMS...

_____

_____

_____

_____

_____

_____

_____

THOUGHTS AND DREAMS...

_____

_____

_____

_____

_____

_____

_____

THOUGHTS AND DREAMS...

_____

_____

_____

_____

_____

_____

_____

THOUGHTS AND DREAMS...

_____

_____

_____

_____

_____

_____

_____

_____

THOUGHTS AND DREAMS...

_____

_____

_____

_____

_____

_____

_____

_____

THOUGHTS AND DREAMS...

_____

_____

_____

_____

_____

_____

_____

THOUGHTS AND DREAMS...

THOUGHTS AND DREAMS...

_____

_____

_____

_____

_____

_____

_____

THOUGHTS AND DREAMS...

_____

_____

_____

_____

_____

_____

_____

THOUGHTS AND DREAMS...

THOUGHTS AND DREAMS...

THOUGHTS AND DREAMS...

_____

_____

_____

_____

_____

_____

_____

THOUGHTS AND DREAMS...

_____

_____

_____

_____

_____

_____

_____

_____

THOUGHTS AND DREAMS...

_____

_____

_____

_____

_____

_____

_____

THOUGHTS AND DREAMS...

THOUGHTS AND DREAMS...

_____

_____

_____

_____

_____

_____

_____

_____

THOUGHTS AND DREAMS...

_____

_____

_____

_____

_____

_____

_____

_____

THOUGHTS AND DREAMS...

_____

_____

_____

_____

_____

_____

_____

THOUGHTS AND DREAMS...

_____

_____

_____

_____

_____

_____

_____

_____

THOUGHTS AND DREAMS...

_____

_____

_____

_____

_____

_____

_____

_____

ABOUT THE AUTHOR

Brandi Edwards is an ambitious and creative soul, who loves everything that has to do with the ARTS. Brandi liked to sing, write poetry, act. In school, English was her favorite subject. Brandi is a natural born leader. In her school days she was the president of the Step Team, Commander of the ROTC Drill team, Captain of the basketball team, and was voted for homecoming court three years in a row.

Brandi is the mom of a ten-year-old boy who she was able to travel to California with, and share her talents of acting and creating. Always having a love for God and the Gospel, Brandi was strongly moved in a spiritual direction when she suffered a huge loss. In that time of darkness, light was revealed, and her first book is a product of that process. Brandi has since started a company "Solemn Creatives" which will focus on all aspects of production, share related products, and eventually be an outlet for other creatives to display their ART around the world.